hampstead theatre

HAMPSTEAD THEATRE PRESENTS THE WORLD PREMIERE OF

When the Night Begins
by Hanif Kureishi

Cast (in order of speaking)

Cecil **Michael Pennington**
Jane **Catherine McCormack**

Director **Anthony Clark**
Designer **Patrick Connellan**
Lighting **Paul Pyant**
Sound **Gregory Clarke**

Fight Director **Terry King**
Casting Director **Siobhan Bracke**
Deputy Stage Manager **Abi Duddleston**
Rehearsal Assistant Stage Manager **Christabel Anderson**
Costume Supervisor **Laura Hunt**
Set constructed by **PGH Scenic Workshop**
Set painted by **Sarah Burton**

Press Representative **Sue Hyman**
sue.hyman@btinternet.com

When the Night Begins was first performed at
Hampstead Theatre on 3 March 2004.

The text that follows was correct at the time
of going to print, but may have changed during rehearsal.

Charity Registration No 218506
Company Registration No 707180
VAT No 230 3818 91

The Company

Hanif Kureishi Writer

Hanif Kureishi's early plays include **Soaking the Heat** (Royal Court Theatre Upstairs, 1976), **The King and Me** (Soho Poly, 1979) and **The Mother Country** (Riverside's Plays Umbrella season, 1980), which won him the Thames Television Playwright Award. In 1981 he became Writer-in-Residence at the Royal Court winning the George Devine Award for his next play, **Outskirts** (Warehouse), shortly followed by **Tomorrow Today** (Soho Poly).

Commissioned by the Joint Stock Company and opening at the Royal Court Theatre in 1981, **Borderline** won both the Thames Television Bursary and Drama Magazine's Award for Most Promising New Playwright. Hanif also co-adapted Janusz Glowacki's play, **Cinders**, for the Royal Court Theatre Upstairs in 1981. With the director, David Leveaux, he translated and adapted a new version of Ostrovsky's **Artists and Admirers** which was presented at the Riverside Studios in 1982. His adaptation for radio of Kafka's **The Trial** was first transmitted in the same year and repeated in 1983.

His stage play, **Birds of Passage,** opened at Hampstead Theatre in 1983, and was directed by Howard Davies who also directed his version of **Mother Courage** at the Barbican at the end of 1984.

His first film (commissioned as a Film on Four), **My Beautiful Laundrette,** won the Evening Standard Award for Best Film 1985, the New York Critics Best Screenplay Award 1986, and received BAFTA and Oscar nominations for Best Screenplay.

His second film, **Sammy and Rosie Get Laid,** was released in 1988. The screenplay, together with his diary record of the film's making, has been published by Faber.

Published in 1990, his novel **The Buddha of Suburbia** won the Whitbread Award for Best First Novel and was subsequently televised for the BBC.

Hanif wrote and directed **London Kills Me,** a feature film for Working Title which opened in 1991.

Hanif's second novel, **The Black Album**, was published in 1995, whilst a collection of short stories, **Love in a Blue Time**, was published in 1997.

In 1998, **My Son The Fanatic,** a feature film which Hanif adapted from his short story, was released.

Intimacy, a novel published in 1999, was filmed by director Patrice Chéreau and starred Mark Rylance and Kerry Fox. A second collection of short stories, **Midnight All Day,** was published in 2000 and a new novel **Gabriel's Gift** in 2001.

Sleep with Me, a stage play, was produced in 1999 at the National Theatre's Cottesloe.

His novel **The Body and Seven Stories** was published in 2002.

The Mother, an original screenplay directed by Roger Michell, won the European Cinema Award at Cannes in 2003.

Hanif's latest novel, **The Ear at his Heart,** will be published by Faber in October.

Catherine McCormack Jane

Theatre includes: **Under the Curse** (Gate Theatre); **Honour, Dinner, Free, All My Sons** - Olivier Award nomination (National Theatre); **White Horses** (The Gate Theatre, Dublin); **Lie of the Mind** (Donmar Warehouse); **Kiss Me Like You Meant It** (Soho Theatre) and **Anna Weiss** (Whitehall Theatre).

Television includes **Gunpowder, Treason and Plot, Armadillo, Deacon Brodie** and **How to Do Love in the 21st Century – Frenzy.**

Film includes **A Sound of Thunder, Spy

Game, Tailor of Panama, Born Romantic, The Weight of Water, A Rumour of Angels, Shadow of the Vampire, The Debtors, This Years'** Love, Dancing at Lughnasa, Land Girls, The Honest Courtesan, Braveheart and Loaded.

Catherine directed the short film **Running to Stand Still,** written by William Boyd.

Michael Pennington Cecil

Theatre includes: **The Madness of George III** (West Yorkshire Playhouse / Birmingham Rep); **The Seagull** (Edinburgh International Festival); **John Gabriel Borkman** (English Touring Theatre); **The Front Page** (Chichester Festival Theatre); **The Shawl** (Sheffield Crucible); **What the Butler Saw** (national tour); **The Guardsman** (Albery Theatre); **Gross Indecency** (Gielgud Theatre); **The Misanthrope, Filumena, Waste, The Provok'd Wife, The Seagull** (Peter Hall season at the Old Vic); **Anton Chekhov** (one man show at the Old Vic & National Theatre); **The Entertainer** (Hampstead Theatre); **Taking Sides** (Criterion Theatre); **Hamlet** (Gielgud Theatre); **Old Times, One for the Road** (Dublin Festival); **Gift of the Gorgon** (Wyndhams Theatre); **The Real Thing** (Strand Theatre); **Crime and Punishment** (Lyric Theatre) and **Strider, Venice Preserved** (National Theatre).

For the Royal Shakespeare Company: **Timon of Athens, Hamlet, Shadow of a Gunman, Hippolytus, Love's Labours Lost, Way of the World, Romeo and Juliet, King Lear, Measure for Measure, Destiny, Playing with Trains, Thirteenth Night** and **Afore Night Come.**

For the English Shakespeare Company (co-founder and joint Artistic Director): **Macbeth, Coriolanus, The Winter's Tale**

and **The Wars of the Roses.**

Directing work includes: **A Midsummer Night's Dream** (Open Air Theatre, Regent's Park); **Twelfth Night** (Chicago Shakespeare Theatre); **Twelfth Night** (Haiyuza Company, Tokyo - Japanese version) and **Twelfth Night** (English Shakespeare Company, world tour).

Film and television includes **State of Play, Waking the Dead, The Dinosaur Hunters, Silent Witness, Dr. Terrible's House of Horrible, Dalziel & Pascoe, Cracker, Kavanagh QC, Between the Lines, Operation Epsilon, Summer's Lease, In My Defense, The Return of Sherlock Holmes, Oedipus Rex, Cymbeline, Return of the Jedi, White Guard, Outside Edge, Waving to a Train, Danton's Death, Mr & Mrs Bureaucrat** and **Mad Jack.**

Published writing: **Hamlet – A User's Guide; Twelfth Night – A User's Guide; Are You There Crocodile – Inventing Chekhov** (all on sale in the foyer) and **The English Shakespeare Company – The Story of the Wars of the Roses.** Writing in preparation: **A Midsummer Night's Dream – A User's Guide.**

Anthony Clark Director

Anthony's recent directing credits include **Revelations** and **The Maths Tutor** (Hampstead Theatre), **Edward III** (RSC), **Krindlekrax** (Nottingham Playhouse), **The Slight Witch** (Birmingham Rep) and **Loveplay** (RSC).

He started his career working with The Orange Tree Theatre and Tara Arts before becoming Artistic Director of Contact Theatre in Manchester, where his favourite productions include: **A Midsummer Night's Dream, The Duchess of Malfi, Blood Wedding** (Manchester Evening News Best Production Award), **Mother Courage and Her Children, Oedipus Rex, To Kill a Mockingbird** (Manchester Evening News Best Production Award) and new plays **Two Wheeled Tricycle, Face Value, Green, Homeland,** and **McAlpine's Fusiliers**. In 1990 he joined Birmingham Repertory Theatre as Associate Artistic Director where he directed **Macbeth, Julius Caesar, Atheist's Tragedy** (TMA Best Director Award), **The Seagull, Of Mice and Men, Threepenny Opera, Saturday Sunday Monday, The Grapes of Wrath, The Playboy of the Western World, Pygmalion, Gentlemen Prefer Blondes** (the play), **St Joan, The Entertainer** and premiere of David Lodge's **Home Truths**.

He was responsible for launching and programming The Door (formerly The Rep Studio), dedicated exclusively to promoting new plays. There he directed **Nervous Women** by Sara Woods, **Rough** by Kate Dean, **True Brit** by Ken Blakeson, **Confidence** by Judy Upton, **Paddy Irishman** by Declan Croghan, **All That Trouble** by Paul Lucas, **Silence** by Moira Buffini, **My Best Friend** by Tamsin Oglesby and **Belonging** by Kaite O'Reilly.

His freelance credits include **Dr Faustus** (Young Vic), **The Red Balloon** (Bristol Old Vic / National Theatre, TMA Best Show for Young People Award), **The Snowman** (Leicester Haymarket), **Mother Courage and Her Children** (National Theatre), **The Day After Tomorrow** (National Theatre), **The Wood Demon** (The Playhouse).

Patrick Connellan Designer

Patrick designed **The Maths Tutor** and **My Best Friend** (Hampstead Theatre / Birmingham Repertory Theatre).

Other London theatre includes: **Edward III** (RSC at the Gielgud Theatre); **The Slight Witch** (National Theatre / Birmingham Repertory Theatre); **Paddy Irishman, Paddy Englishman, Paddy...** (Tricycle Theatre / Birmingham); **Perfect Days** (Greenwich Theatre / Wolsey Theatre, Ipswich); **A Passionate Woman** (Comedy Theatre); **Misery** (Criterion Theatre) and **Salad Days** (Vaudeville Theatre).

Other theatre design also includes: **Little Malcolm and his Struggle Against the Eunuchs, The Weir, Ham!, The Hypochondriac, Miss Julie, The Blue Room** (Bolton Octagon); **The Rink, A Midsummer Night's Dream** (also associate director), **The Dice House** (Belgrade Theatre, Coventry); **Heaven Can Wait** (No 1 tour); **Leader of the Pack** (No 1 tour); **The Marriage of Figaro** (New Vic, Stoke / Scarborough); **Morning Glory** (Birmingham Repertory Theatre / Watford Palace / Cambridge Arts); **St Joan, Julius Caesar, The Atheist's Tragedy, Down Red Lane, Pygmalion, The Grapes Of Wrath** (Birmingham Repertory Theatre); **Coriolanus, When We Are Married, The Rivals** (West Yorkshire Playhouse); **The Wizard Of Oz** (set, Leicester Haymarket); **A View From The Bridge** (Harrogate Theatre); **A Passionate Woman** (Gloria Theatre, Athens) and **A Midsummer Night's Dream, She Knows You Know** (New Vic Theatre).

He directed and designed **This Limetree Bower** (Belgrade Theatre, Coventry / Edinburgh Festival) last summer and is about to direct and design **Popcorn** (Octagon Theatre, Bolton).

Paul Pyant Lighting

Paul is a graduate and associate of the Royal Academy of Dramatic Art in London. He has long associations with Glyndebourne Opera, English National Opera, the Royal Opera Covent Garden, the National Theatre, English National Ballet and Northern Ballet Theatre. Theatre includes productions for the RSC, the Donmar Warehouse, West End and Broadway.

Opera includes productions in America (Metropolitan Opera, Los Angeles, Houston, Seattle, Chicago, San Francisco), Australia, New Zealand, Israel, Austria, Japan, France and Italy.

Ballet includes productions with the Norwegian National Ballet, Boston Ballet, Atlanta Ballet and the Royal New Zealand Ballet.

Gregory Clarke Sound

Gregory's sound design credits include: **Journey's End** (The Comedy Theatre); **Betrayal** (The Duchess Theatre); **Abigail's Party** (The New Ambassadors / Whitehall Theatres), **Mum's The Word** (Albery Theatre), **Lady Windermere's Fan, The Royal Family** (Theatre Royal, Haymarket), **Song Of Singapore** (Mayfair Theatre, London) and **No Man's Land** (National Theatre).

For the Royal Shakespeare Company: **Merry Wives of Windsor** (The Old Vic / Stratford / USA Tour); **Coriolanus** (The Old Vic / Stratford) and **Tantalus** (Stratford / UK tour).

Other theatre includes: **The Two Gentlemen of Verona, Loves Labour's Lost** (Open Air Theatre, Regent's Park); **Revelations, Meteorite, The Maths Tutor, Abigail's Party, The Dead Eye Boy, Snake, Gone To LA, Terracotta, Local Boy, Buried Alive, Tender** (Hampstead Theatre);

Semi-Detached, Pal Joey, Heartbreak House, A Small Family Business (Chichester Festival Theatre); **The Cherry Orchard, Demons and Dybbuks, The Black Dahlia** (Method and Madness); **I Caught My Death In Venice, Nathan The Wise, Song of Singapore, Nymph Errant** (Minerva Theatre, Chichester); **Design for Living, Betrayal, Fight for Barbara, As You Like It** (The Peter Hall Company Season at the Theatre Royal Bath); **As You Like It** (US national tour); **Office Suite, Present Laughter** (Theatre Royal Bath); the new musical **Baiju Bawra** (Theatre Royal, Stratford East); **Dick Whittington** (Stratford East at Greenwich); **Krindlekrax** (Birmingham Repertory); **The Hackney Office** (Druid Theatre, Galway); **Beyond A Joke** (Yvonne Arnaud Theatre, co-design with John Leonard) and **Dumped, A Midsummer Night's Dream** (National Youth Theatre).

Hampstead Theatre moved into its new RIBA award winning building in February 2003 after over 40 years in a portacabin that was only expected to last for 10 years.

A theatre dedicated to new writing, in our first year we have presented 8 World premieres, 2 British premieres and 2 London premieres.

Conferencing & Events

Our new building is a stunning venue for celebrations or conferences. For more information talk to us on 020 7034 4914 or email conferencing@hampsteadtheatre.com

Education & Participation Programme

Since its inception in 1998, we have had over 60,000 attendances from aspiring writers and actors aged 5 to 85. Our new home houses a large, dedicated education studio, The Space, which can be transformed from a workshop into a fully equipped performance studio with ease and speed. Local residents and schools are encouraged to make use of the Theatre's expertise and facilities through a number of different projects. To find out more visit our website, talk to us on 020 7449 4165 or email education@hampsteadtheatre.com

Start Nights

A great chance to see the talent of the future flexing its creative muscle. Start Nights are also an opportunity to present twenty minutes of new material to an audience and gauge their feedback. Anyone over the age of 16 living, working or studying in London can participate. Ask at our box office for entry details or check our website.

Start Nights are sponsored by Habitat with support from Arts & Business New Partners.

Cafébar

Open 9.00am – 11.00pm Monday to Saturday, the cafébar offers a generous lunchtime selection of sandwiches, baguettes, warm paninis, pasta and salads. In the evening sandwiches, paninis & snacks are also available or you can order a pre or post show meal by calling us on 020 7722 9301. Check our website for more information.

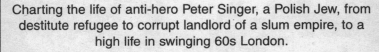
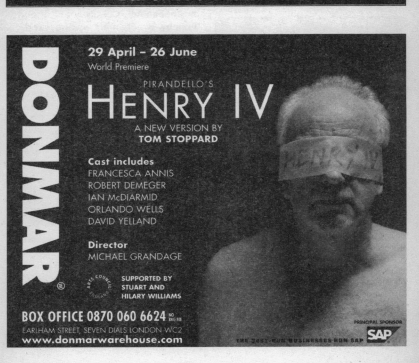

Celebrating one year in our new home, 2003 / 2004

born bad
by debbie tucker green
'Exquisite. The acting is spot on.
tucker green is a distinctive talent'
THE GUARDIAN

In Arabia, We'd All Be Kings
by Stephen Adly Guirgis
'Punchy, street-smart writing – and
excellent performances'
THE INDEPENDENT

Fragile Land
by Tanika Gupta
'Vigorous, vivid and streetwise'
THE DAILY TELEGRAPH

US and Them
by Tamsin Oglesby
'The funniest new comedy for over a
year – unnerving in how fearlessly it
goes for its target. US and Them
doesn't just touch a nerve, it bravely
blasts away at it'
FINANCIAL TIMES

The Maths Tutor
by Clare McIntyre
'Anthony Clark's sensitive, absorbing
production is undoubtedly a fine start
to his regime as Hampstead's new
artistic director'
THE DAILY TELEGRAPH

Revelations
by Stephen Lowe
'Lowe is a fine writer and Anthony
Clark's production is both superbly
acted and genuinely thought-
provoking'
THE DAILY MAIL

Awards

Royal Institute of British Architects Award
2003

ADAPT Trust Access Award 2003 -
Barry Foster Memorial Award

Evening Standard Outstanding Newcomer
Award - Tom Hardy for his performance in
In Arabia, We'd All Be Kings

Award nominations

Laurence Olivier Outstanding Achievement
Award nomination -
Tanika Gupta for **Fragile Land** at
Hampstead Theatre and her adaptation of
Hobson's Choice at the Young Vic

Laurence Olivier Most Promising Newcomer
Award nomination -
debbie tucker green for **born bad**

Laurence Olivier Most Promising Newcomer
Award nomination -
Tom Hardy for his performance in **In
Arabia, We'd All Be Kings**

The Straits
by Gregory Burke
'This engrossing new play brilliantly
captures how the political is personal'
THE DAILY TELEGRAPH

hampstead theatre

Supporting Hampstead Theatre

Priority Supporters
With advance information and priority booking you can be the first to discover fresh and dynamic playwrights, and make the most of a whole range of discounts for just £12 a year. For more details call us on 020 7722 9301 or email info@hampsteadtheatre.com

Luminaries
By becoming one of Hampstead Theatre's Luminaries, you will be giving vital support to all aspects of our work, and become more involved with the theatre. There are three levels of support and a variety of benefits offered including priority booking, a dedicated booking line, crediting in playtexts and programmes and invitations to exclusive events. Membership starts at £250 per year.

Our current Luminaries are:

Level 1
Anonymous, Michael & Leslie Bennett, Deborah Buzan, Denis & Ronda Cassidy, Sir Trevor Chinn, Richard Curtis, Frankie de Freitas, Robyn Durie, George Fokschaner, Richard Gladstone, Elaine & Peter Hallgarten, Lew Hodges, Patricia & Jerome Karet, Richard & Ariella Lister, Tom & Karen Mautner, Judith Mishon & Philip Mishon OBE, Sandy & David Montague, Trevor Phillips, Tamara & Michael Rabin, Peter Roth QC, Barry Serjent, Dr Michael Spiro, Marmont Management Ltd. Hugh Whitemore & Rohan McCulloch, Dr Adrian Whiteson & Mrs Myrna Whiteson and Peter Williams

Level 2
Dorothy & John Brook, Professor & Mrs C J Dickinson, David Dutton, Matthew & Alison Green, The Mackintosh Foundation, Midge & Simon Palley, Michael & Olivia Prior, Anthony Rosner and Judy Williams

Level 3
Jacqueline and Jonathan Gestetner, Sir Eddie Kulukundis OBE , Daniel Peltz , Richard Peskin, Wendy and Peter Phillips and Paul Rayden

Corporate Partners
Hampstead Theatre is proud to launch its Corporate Partners scheme. This offers a flexible package of benefits with which you can entertain your clients, promote your business objectives and take advantage of everything that the new theatre has to offer. Corporate Partners membership is available from £5,000 + VAT.

Our current Corporate Partners are:

Bennetts Associates Architects

habitat

SOLOMON TAYLOR & SHAW SOLICITORS

THOMSON
SWEET & MAXWELL

CHAMPAGNE
TAITTINGER
Reims

We offer a range of other sponsorship opportunities, from performance sponsorship, project support, production sponsorship, gala event sponsorship, education support or even title sponsorship for the entire season. Benefits can be tailored to your needs – please talk to us for more information.

Support Us

If there is a particular area of our work that you would like to support, please talk to us. We have numerous projects available covering all aspects of our work from education to play development.

As a registered charity, Hampstead Theatre can accept donations from charitable trusts and foundations, gifts of stocks and shares, donations via CAF America or in a tax-efficient manner under the Gift Aid scheme. Making the declaration is simple – contact the Development team for more information.

Legacies

Why not consider leaving a legacy to the theatre? This gives us lasting support well into the future. You can leave a gift to support a new commission, to fund education work or leave it open for us to use it in the area of most need.

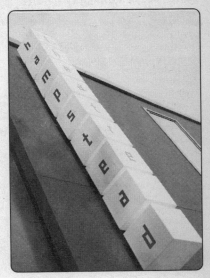

Naming Seats

We have released the remaining seats in the auditorium of the new theatre to be named. The seats in the initial batch were all named before the new theatre opened in February 2003. Why not name a seat after yourself, your children, in memory of a loved one or to promote your business? Seats are available from £1,500 and payments can be spread over 3 years.

Hampstead Theatre's Supporters
2003/04

Abbey National Charitable Foundation – Supporting Sign Interpreted Performances
ADAPT Trust – Barry Foster Memorial Award for Excellence in Access, 2003
Arts & Business New Partners
Auerbach Trust Charity
Bridge House Estates Trust Fund
Champagne Taittinger
The City Parochial Foundation
The Clothworkers Foundation
Deutsche Ag Bank
John Lyon's Charitable Trust
The John S Cohen Foundation
Lloyds TSB Foundation for England and Wales
Mildred Duveen Trust
The Rayne Foundation
Reed Elsevier

For more information on any of these or if you would like to support the theatre in another way, please contact Antonia Nicol in the Development Department on 020 7449 4160 or email development@hampsteadtheatre.com

When the Night Begins

HANIF KUREISHI

When the Night Begins

faber and faber

First published in 2004
by Faber and Faber Limited
3 Queen Square London WCIN 3AU

Typeset by Country Setting, Kingsdown, Kent CT14 8ES
Printed in England by Mackays of Chatham plc, Chatham, Kent

A CIP record for this book
is available from the British Library

ISBN 0–571–22448–2

2 4 6 8 10 9 7 5 3 1

Characters

Jane
mid-thirties

Cecil
mid-late sixties

WHEN THE NIGHT BEGINS

Cecil's flat, Streatham.

Cecil (*off*) You see what I mean about these stairs . . .
Sorry about the lift . . . but keep going, it'll be good for
you . . . If I can do it day after day, you can, with your
strong legs . . . Long as you don't forget the milk . . .
which I always do . . . You haven't left anything behind,
have you? Are you sure?

He enters.

It's not far now . . . up you come . . . you're doing well . .
. come in . . . come right on in, Jane, to my little place,
my eyrie, my hideaway –

She enters.

What a surprise this is. You are so welcome . . . this is
beautiful . . . a lovely moment and a treat for me . . .
(*Pause.*) What are you doing down here, walking about
my area . . . sitting in my local café, almost opposite
me . . .? How much of that greasy tea did you get down
before you spoke to me? Were you there a while?

Jane It was some time –

Cecil Taking me all in, Jane, sizing me up. Nice little
café, eh? I go there for breakfast and I usually pop in
during the day. They know me and what I like, lucky
them. You know I don't like to cook for one. Let me take
your coat. Your glasses? No? We'll keep the lights on
then. (*Pause.*) Can you stay long? A couple of hours?
(*Pause.*) I don't think I would have recognised you . . .
I haven't been at all well, my eyes are on the blink, along

9

with my arms, legs, brain . . . Did you get my Christmas cards?

Jane Yes.

Cecil Long as they went to the right place. (*Pause.*) There was a photograph of you in the paper, when your husband died. You don't even look like that now . . .

Jane Don't I?

Cecil Well it was only your head. You're much more graceful. More elegant, all over. You used to practise your walk – up and down, up and down, in front of the mirror. That's the one. It's you now. Strange how that can happen. Have you become her, that woman, at last, the one you pretended to be? I'm not sure. (*Pause.*) Oh . . . Christ. There isn't a lot here, compared to what you're used to . . . I'd move, if it weren't for the happy memories. People don't drop in, no one vital wants to see an old 'un, except my mates from the buses. But, you know, they're from the union, as you used to point out, with limited points of view. Cup of tea?

Jane No . . . no.

Cecil Would you like water? I know some people these days won't touch it from the tap – still or sparkling, they say – there's nothing sparkling in here –

Jane It's all right.

Cecil Still or sparkling, reminds me, someone told me – your mother, I think it was –

Jane Mum?

Cecil Bumped into Esther on the street, this is a long while back, we didn't talk, God no, at least I didn't. Anyway, I knew Bernard had died, what, two years ago? It was on a news programme. A second stroke. He was ill, wasn't he, more than a year of –

Jane Yes –

Cecil – suffering . . . nursing, close attention. There was a lot . . . they wrote pages of good things about his films. I cut them out in case you were too grieved to see. You can look through them later, or just take them. I've seen all his films now, except the early documentaries.

Jane Really?

Cecil Have you seen them? Brilliant man, lived a fulfilled life, was without bitterness, we liked the same kind of music. What was he, eighteen years older than you –

Jane About that.

Cecil I guess his other children were grown up. They'd left home. Didn't he have a couple of ex-wives?

Jane (*looks in her bag*) I've got some water.

Cecil That looks good. I am going to have a drink with you.

Jane Cecil – wait –

He fetches a beer.

Cecil I'm parched. It's been a hot summer. But it's already getting dark. Not that those blinds let in much light. I wouldn't begin to know how to clean venetian blinds . . . I don't open the windows because of the traffic noise. And the neighbours screaming. Is there an old-man stink?

Jane Maybe. It's . . . it's . . .

Cecil Sultry. Is that the word? We need some rain. Didn't you have the address? (*Pause.*) You did come here, you know, when I'd just moved in, to drop off a couple of my old suits. You were staying with your boyfriend, that local lad. I still drink with his old man. You made him wait across the road, minding your bicycle. You were at college, must have been twenty – That was the last time you saw me. How old were you when you met your husband?

Jane Twenty-two.

Cecil Twenty-two. You. Remind me of how you got to know him.

Jane Someone got me a little job on one of his films. They call them runners.

Cecil Yeah? And he picked you out? Or did you pick him out? A bit of both?

Jane He was intrigued that I had a group. He asked us to play at the wrap party. Said he liked the way I worked the bass but thought I should sing. So I did.

Cecil So you did. You just sang and you danced. (*Pause.*) Now. This is the moment. It's been too long.

Jane I'm glad you're alive, Cecil.

Cecil Are you? Me too, baby. How about it? Let's say hello, let's celebrate while we can. To you, Jane, as always, your glory, happiness, strength and wealth –

He tears open a can of lager.

Jane Please don't –

Cecil You are all quality now, Jane, I can see that. She's classy, we'd say. She can read the menu and even understand all the foreign words. (*Pause.*) You want something. Is that it? Or is something bothering you? Are you in bad trouble?

Jane You can see I am, can't you?

Cecil Yes, I'm afraid I can. Say what it is, girl. You can talk here, everyone does.

Jane Everyone?

Cecil Yeah.

Jane I have been away for some time.

Cecil Have you?

Jane Working – painting – in Venice. A friend let me have their studio . . . I have an exhibition coming up. My first, yes. It's really only a few weeks away, in an arts centre, a couple of miles from here, in fact.

Cecil There wouldn't be much traffic noise in Venice –

Jane (*pause*) It's not much, the exhibition, it's in the foyer of the place, a corridor, really –

Cecil Doesn't matter. It's on. What are they?

Jane Portraits, which I do from photographs. Or sometimes, if they have time, the people sit for me, which I prefer.

Cecil I could sit. I've had a lot of practice. I could sit still and still sparkle! Aren't I handsome enough? But good, good – Who?

Jane My husband of course, from memory, a couple of actors and musicians, a model, a writer, a politician –

Cecil All close friends who come to the house for drinks?

Jane Some.

Cecil Oh, I need to see this work.

Jane One day I want to call myself a painter.

Cecil Yeah? You will. That is good, daughter. It is so –

Jane Sorry?

Cecil . . . fortifying, to see you coming on like this, painter now – I don't suppose you do any decorating?

Pause.

Jane Dad died, I was five. You came to us, what was I, twelve –

Cecil Thirteen –

Jane Little Jimmy was still in the juniors – I cannot, will not, be called a . . . I was never your daughter.

Cecil I'm gasping. I will have that drink, loosen my goose.

He drinks. She moves the can.

Jane In Venice, when it starts to get dark, and the place begins to seems quite eerie, and I –

Cecil Sorry, I have to know, forgive me, just this one thing, we've got time, haven't we, before you say what it is?

Jane Yes?

Cecil What did Bernard leave you? The house in town, of course, another in the country, with the stables and pool – I've seen it in the magazines. Garages, rugs, paintings, dinners. Quiet foreign people to lay the tables, to garden, cook, clean. Is there a large staff? D'you run it all yourself? There must be other places –

Jane A flat in Los Angeles. I forget.

Cecil I know you do. You're still a young 'un and set for life. What we used to call a 'multi' – Remember? You're a 'multi-millionaire'.

Jane From the beginning Bernard prepared me for the envy. People will not be entirely happy for you, he said, with all that you will have. Even self-envy, that I didn't deserve it – Nobody from nowhere.

Cecil But you deal with it? Yes. And the little girl is used to it, brought up with nannies, piano teachers and orthodontists from day one –

Jane While I've been painting, Emily has been visiting in the mountains, with my boyfriend –

Cecil Really?

Jane She and I have never been apart for so long.

Cecil She can take it, you both can.

Jane Yes. It's good for us.

Cecil But the man, what does he do? Is he new?

Jane Mum adores Emily, Cecil. (*Pause.*) Mother and I get along for hours at a time now without wanting to mutilate one another . . . She comes to the house almost every fortnight. (*Pause.*) I'd been doing my widow's work, getting Bernard's letters, scripts and journals to the Institute. Next year I will edit his film workbooks. Mum, Emily and I went to America for a break. I took a house on the beach. You know, Mum was an absolute delight, insofar as a mother is ever a delight. Emily surfs like a dancer. She made Mum swim in the sea –

Cecil Esther swimming?

Jane Well, floating – on her back – Not much effort. I think she was surprised to be held up.

Cecil If only I could have seen it!

Jane Mum and I took yoga and shiatsu classes. Mum even cooked, yes, and talked to people she hadn't met –

Cecil No –

Jane She seemed open at last, and joyful, and, well, you know, she'd never been anywhere much. Before, she'd hitch-hike at random, waiting at the end of the road, trying to make spontaneity, until she had to be fetched from some field where she'd heard the mushrooms were magic. But outside England –

Cecil And all paid for –

Jane Never.

Cecil Most people don't have that chance –

Jane No.

Cecil I was going to say, if you don't mind me saying, while you're in Venice, you could have left Emily with her, with Esther –

Jane We go slowly, Mum and I, we sort of circle each other. She finds me difficult, she says, which pleases me, pleases me more than anything. I was always too easy. Isn't that right? Pushed into being the responsible one. But Emily has stayed with her –

Cecil In the house? In your old bedroom? Beautiful – The two of them, talking away the night – She's bright, bright –

Jane Who?

Cecil A dazzling, uncommon child, your daughter. Jane, she must be, surely, coming from you . . .

> *Pause.*

Jane In Venice –

Cecil Yes – Right.

Jane Where people tell you endlessly that the glass mirror was re-invented in the thirteenth century, there are reflections everywhere. I have been alone, days and days, for the first time in years. Walking, eating, and photographing the Venetians who work in the hotels. And I've been writing my journal. Thoughts, dreams, memories . . . stories. Trying to get acquainted with myself again. Have you ever known that wish?

Cecil No.

Jane And at night I've been painting – learning to – thinking about these faces and flesh and bodies. Seeing what I can do. I've got to work fast now, I'm so behind –

Cecil But I've got to say here, go as slowly as you can, Jane –

Jane Yes –

Cecil I know what a hurrier you can be . . . racing into the future before you're ready . . . I always said –

Jane I've had insomnia since I was a teenager, sometimes I'm up two nights, pacing . . . Anyhow, I could not look at the photographs of the adults without thinking of them as children. I looked at portraits by other artists – Soutine, Caravaggio – but all I could see was that the subjects had suffered. I returned to a self-portrait I was working on, in dark colours, with my knees up, holding a book. As I sat in front of the mirror I heard whispering . . . voices telling me I am worthless, a nothing, a void, a mistake –

Cecil No –

Jane As my self-belief shattered, my face began to slip and break up too. There was someone else there . . .

Cecil What kind of someone else?

Jane It was you. You as a ghost, and then more palpably, your eyes, face, fingers, your body, which forced itself, over and over, into my mind.

Cecil Me? Good, good. I have been a little bit annoyed, to be straight, that you haven't been in touch, Jane –

Jane I'm sorry?

Cecil Thought you might be interested to know, I'm retired and read slowly, I want to understand now, biography, history, poetry –

Jane There was nothing holding me together –

Cecil It's late for me to alter but I go on, the library's not bad, though you have to wait a bit –

Jane My therapist had led me back, but I couldn't turn off the madness – the flashing in my mind increased –

Cecil Therapist? Like a psychiatrist? How many times have you had to go?

Jane It's twice or three times a week, when I'm in town. Seven years.

Cecil You went to a stranger, Jane, for guidance, and they did this to you? What did they charge?

Jane I don't expect a cure. I only want to live with myself, to live better, yes. But I can't do that yet. I covered the mirrors with sheets, but I was pacing . . . night after night, and not working. In the end I decided to speak. You know Mother didn't like people talking too much. I left the studio, took the vaporetto and a plane, and came here. You see, I want you to speak.

Cecil In the library round the corner they have music, which settles me, you know I love the blues, so did Bernard, we had similar backgrounds in fact, anything poignant – I'll play a record.

Jane Not now –

Cecil Jane, they'll be listening to Billie and Bessie on the last day of the world. I've learned a lot recently, grasped some things –

Jane But you cannot have a drink.

Cecil No wallop? Not even in my own hole?

Jane You haven't changed. When was the last time you went a day without –

Cecil Can't remember.

Jane How much do you remember, Cecil?

Cecil Of what? I'm getting on a bit now. Things slip.

Jane Let's be here together tonight, then –

Cecil Right-oh.

Jane And go through some things that still seem to matter . . .

Cecil Let's. We'll go through them, but I cannot guarantee anything, my brain's shot to pieces –

Jane If there's enough detail, something might occur.

Cecil Facts and figures, eh? They might occur. They might not. That is my point. What if they just don't?

Jane You might need a hint. You could be prompted.

Cecil How?

Jane Oh, that'll be a surprise.

Cecil Will it? I like surprises. But not shocks. No. And this is already sudden – You didn't say –

Jane I know – You're not ready, not prepared.

Cecil No.

Jane I can assure you, that's really for the best.

Cecil Is it? It's good, though, great to see you. (*Pause.*) I think I might have a camomile tea somewhere. Or nettle.

Jane Don't worry.

Cecil D'you want me to look? I should give you something. I want to. If you've been feeling funny, it'll relax you.

   He looks in a cupboard.

19

Jane It'll take more than a cup of tea to relax me.

Cecil You wait . . . Nettle, camomile, nettle, rose-hip . . . Chocolate? Nettle, nettle . . . You like to be close to nature, eh? You don't want anything real?

Jane Like what?

Cecil Instant coffee? Personally I just sprinkle it on my tongue and let my spit do the rest.

Jane Cecil, I haven't asked for anything.

Cecil Yes you have. By coming here, you have awakened my hospitality. You will see me do what I can for you.

The front-door buzzer sounds.

Jane Jesus, who the fuck's that? Cecil –

Cecil Wait. Let me fucking see.

Jane No. Don't go anywhere.

Cecil What? Why not?

Jane Didn't you used to have lodgers?

Cecil Students from the nursing college, sometimes. Those girls would pour nettles down their throats, amongst other things –

Jane Tell them to go away.

Cecil But there's no one staying at the moment.

The buzzer sounds again.

Jane Leave it. Cecil, please. It's just us.

Cecil You were always a bossy little miss. Just hold on will you a minute, Jane. Let me sort this out, I'll get your tea and we can get on with what we were saying. Or you can come back another day.

Jane No!

Cecil Now you've remembered where I am, there'll be other opportunities.

Jane I don't want anyone else here! I am . . . determined!

Cecil This isn't your place! Remember who's the boss, if you don't mind, yeah?

> *She takes a knife out of her bag.*

Cecil Jesus, what are you playing at?

Jane Cecil –

Cecil Okay, okay. (*Pause.*) What's happened to you?

Jane I don't know. It's not good.

Cecil No, it doesn't look promising.

Jane With you, at all times, I must be protected. You have to sit.

Cecil You should too. But yes, I will do that. Right. Is this sitting . . . okay?

Jane My therapist says that everything that happens has happened before. We are like rats on a wheel, going round and round, choiceless, unless there is knowledge, unless there is understanding. (*Pause.*) Years ago it came to me, what I should do. I've carried it since, this important job. I've always known it had to be done. D'you see?

Cecil I do, yes, yes. I do see now. (*Pause.*) I like an argument, a fight over truth, the working-class movement has been my whole life . . . The people I have helped and others who have heard about me, the unemployed, the exploited, maltreated. They still come for advice and courage. I cannot be frightened. But Jane, I know you wouldn't hurt anyone if you could be blamed for it.

She smashes his head down on the table.

Cecil You hurt me. Ow . . . Jesus, Jane, what's made you so vicious?

Jane You. You.

The buzzer sounds.

Cecil Look . . . look . . . Jane . . . Jane . . . don't worry, I am not moving . . . an inch.

Jane Will they come in?

Cecil No, no – How can they?

Jane I'm panicked now, and if they do come through that door – bam!

The buzzer sounds.

Cecil It's no one . . . they ring all the bells, the kids –

Jane Kids? Who – who – who is it really! They're going to get it –

Cecil It's only your mother, Esther.

Jane No. No. You're joking.

Cecil No.

Jane What does she want? Mother . . . Mother . . . Cecil – what?

Pause.

Cecil Take it easy. You sit down. Come on. You'll cut yourself in a minute. (*Pause.*) She's walking away now, in her summer raincoat and that moulting wig she's got to wear now. Looking back, all confused, wondering where I am, what's going on – That's the truth. Who's to say she won't turn round and come back? She'll be worrying about my condition. She was going to see to my eyes. Bathe them and make me feel so good.

Jane You see her. (*Pause.*) I can move quickly. (*Pause.*) How often! Every month? Every week? Every few minutes –

Cecil Okay, okay.

Jane So –

Cecil All the time.

Jane Since – Since –

Cecil Since for ever. Not long after you ran, I moved out of the house and got this place. Had to. My blood pressure's in the thousands and she's getting madder. I can't cope with her. She attacked me and I thought, that's it, the end. Sanity's definitely my favourite quality in a woman. A few days later she's round here, grilling plain fish as though she hadn't come at me with a dustbin lid while I'm in bed. I wouldn't live with her again. Not seeing her can be a real pleasure –

Jane Do you know why she comes to you?

Cecil Don't you know? Can't you see?

Jane No – But I will punch you –

Cecil We only have a cider and some crackers about four times a week. We watch the comedies or she reads to me. We've started on the books together, though her voice can slur, you know, and there's a sort of whistling noise through her old teeth. But I can make out what she's on about – (*He imitates.*) 'Once upon a time there was a little girl who lived in the forest –'

Jane Ohhhh . . . You make love? Yes?

Cecil I wouldn't linger on that picture. Since Esther had the lump removed, and she lost her hair, she likes to be held, and I caress her head and rub her legs. That poor old woman – I'm all she's got.

Jane And me and Emily and her son, Jimmy. (*Pause.*) So she lied and lied and lied and –

Cecil Saying what?

Jane She never saw you, you repel and disgust her, she hates you now –

Cecil She does? She didn't say anything like that to me.

Jane No?

Cecil She wouldn't have not mentioned it –

Jane Keep still –

Cecil What are you doing?

Jane You better –

Cecil I will. Moving's a nuisance anyway.

Jane Smelling you –

Cecil What can I do, she can't help loving me, more than she loved your father or any of the other men, more than she loves you or anyone – do you see that? That's called –

Jane What?

Cecil Romantic love.

Jane Your shaving foam –

Cecil You know what she told me? This'll make you laugh. A little bit of a fashionable snob you've become, eating rocket salad and, what did she say, buffalo mozzarella! Do you eat buffalo mozzarella? Have you knowingly given buffalo mozzarella to others? In here we cry laughing. Every day, from America, she rang to say she wanted to be with me –

Jane Did she really? Your hair cream, sweat, it's still the same –

Cecil Oh Jane, how much you have forgotten.

Jane But I haven't now. It's in me!

Cecil You played with my hair and lay on my chest, hold me, Daddy, cuddle me, Daddy, can I put my new dress on for you, Daddy – Did you tell the psychiatrist that? I'll say it to him, if you give me his number –

Jane Mum sat Jimmy and I down and announced we were getting a new father . . . I could hardly remember the real one . . . Can you imagine my excitement and hope? . . . Who is it? What's his name? But you know him already, she said. It was you. You. (*Pause.*) How could I ever have Mum near my daughter now?

Cecil Please, Jane, don't do that to her now –

Jane She knows my determination, and she's done that –

Cecil She's crazy – you're crazy, Jane – but catch her in the right mood and she's safe. I'll guarantee Esther all the way up.

Jane You?

Cecil Girl, don't be too simple here, all she did was put herself before you –

Jane We are herself. Aren't we?

Cecil Buffalo mozzarella – Eat it or ride it? Whoever you are – and I don't know you now, you won't let me – you can't come charging around down here. It's too rough for you, they're thieves with knives and worse. Yesterday I had a bottle flung at me. You live in another world now.

Jane Only just. After college, Mother expected me to go on the dole. At her most inspired moment she did suggest I become a DJ.

Pause.

Before, in the house, there was a day, I went to her, all brave. She was smoking in her chair in the yard, with that lot she hung with. I said, Cecil hurts us too much, we can't take any more. She smirked and asked me to fetch some booze. I went back and told her: when you're passed out on the kitchen floor, or describing your astral visions to that jerk who never takes off the cloak, where do you think the boring bus driver is?

Cecil Jesus, you'll have me eyes out like winkles – -

Jane Where? Where! That got her to her feet. She hit me, called me slapper, prostitute. She was jealous, she was all for slashing you –

Cecil For me – listen! – one of the pleasures of my life was to sit with you at the desk I bought, at your schoolwork –

Jane She threw everyone out and spoke to you, is that right –

Cecil You were quick, you talked, your mind opened as I took you round London on my day off. Museums, the pictures, theatre, people buried up to their necks. 'Spool!' Julie Walters! Such stuff we saw together, you in your tops and dresses and heels . . . You drew, you wrote songs and played guitar and danced – I'd never seen that before, how someone can get so absorbed in you, so hungry for you and listening to everything –

Jane All right, all right, you did your duty –

Cecil You say that! The kids you grew up with, do you see them?– No – every day they walk past the café, looking three times your age with their tribes of yapping, mongrel children . . .

Jane I will not get distracted here –

26

Cecil Out there, they're liars, lunatics, thieves, addicts, they can't buy the highest quality physical and mental health. Not a single one can go to Venice to paint –

Jane Keep on track. What did Mother say?

Cecil Little girl, she knew decent fathers are thin on the ground –

Jane Did you deny it?

Cecil She knew it was true, she believed you –

Jane She did? Good, good.

Cecil There was no dispute. I told her –

Jane What?

Cecil Straight up, I faced her, it went right back to her, if she loved me the way I needed to what reason would there be for me to go anywhere else?

Jane That was all?

Cecil It worked a treat. She slipped on her sling-backs, found a clean dress under the bed, and we went out to the Café de Paris, the local one –

Jane Jesus, man, I thought you'd be packing your bag with her foot up your arse. Instead the two of you had a fish-and-chip supper leaving us with nothing in the house.

He adjusts his cowboy belt.

Cecil Still, you don't look bad on it, do you? There's worse-lookers than you.

Jane It was always the night, Cecil, when the night began so did the fear – I'd been brave, but what did it bring me?

Pause.

Cecil There is pressure in here – D'you mind? I've got to pee. Swollen prostate and it hurts. I can't make it out the bathroom window –

Jane Piss yourself. I think you should just piss yourself. (*Pause.*) You took that belt off to Jimmy, he was so little and thin, slowly like a stripper, 'Get ready, children –'

Cecil Stripper, you would know, aged seventeen and a half, in that filthy pub, opening your legs, the men from the factory dropping change in a beer glass. People I knew, Jesus. Who had to come down there to haul you out and send you to college? The boss took out his knife but I knew in a year you'd have been selling it. Did you thank me? You could thank me now, Jane.

Jane He's never recovered, addict, he does nothing, he can hardly speak –

Cecil Your brother was always half-gone already, miserable, insulting – What d'you think this house is? I'd say, a rest home for the young –

Jane He wasn't yours to hurt –

Cecil I notice . . . I notice you didn't stay behind one minute to care for him or for her – In the end everyone left her.

Jane My mind had been set on the future . . . it was all I saw, and when the time came –

Cecil Your ruthlessness, where did you get that, I wonder –

Jane I was on the train, away to London –

Cecil I recommended it all along, you know that –

Jane One time, she was two, I was swinging Emily, she slipped and broke her arm. I nearly killed myself with self-reproach, and so I can only say, where do you find it in yourself to hurt a child?

Cecil You don't read history, Jane, how children have been brought up, amongst more than twelve siblings, half of which would die, then the mother would die and the stepmother throw them on the street . . . it was a stew of fucking and dirt and disease and despair. Those Raphaels you've been studying have given you the wrong idea 'bout what goes on . . . Let me pee, Jane, or are you going to kill me first?

Jane When you had your boots on the whole house shook. You could kick a door in.

Cecil I did –

Jane Now you're old, Cecil –

Cecil At least you pity me –

Jane Memory saves me the trouble of that.

Cecil Jane –

Jane I'd lie in bed, boiling in layers of clothes, listening to the stoned, aggressive voices of nonsense. Then I'd make out your footsteps, my door would open, the sound of that belt . . . and your breathing . . . your body and how you made me put my arms around you? Do you remember how many times it was? Did you think that it hurt? That it would cut and bruise for ever? To get out of the house I'd sometimes go to church. (*Pause.*) Cecil, I learned that for the wrong that people do, there will be a weighing hour . . . and that is tonight.

Cecil Who owns the scales? A man's life doesn't boil down to a few nights –

Jane Doesn't it?

Cecil It can't, Jane. There are years of other things . . . There has to be. Give me the chance to say, to explain, to speak . . . Please, will you? I beg you to hear certain facts.

Isn't that what you've come for? Or are you scared of the truth? (*Pause.*) I've got to go right now. Excuse me. I'll leave the door open in case you need to know exactly where I am –

>   *He goes into the bathroom.*
>   *Pause. The phone rings.*

(*off*) Always, when you pee! You can count on it! If I want someone to call, I pee! Jane! Jane! Can you –

>   *She cuts the phone cord.*

(*off*) Who is it? Is that her? What are you telling her? I'm just coming! Fuck, it's going down my leg.

>   *She walks about the room. Pause. She finds the*
>   *chocolate he offered earlier, and eats it. She waits for*
>   *him. Pause. After a while:*

Jane Cecil. Time's up . . .

Cecil (*off*) Jesus, can't you just wait five minutes for an old man's dribble –

Jane Cecil, I'm coming in –

Cecil (*off*) But I'm coming out –

>   *Pause. He comes screaming out of the bathroom with*
>   *the belt in his hand, which he smashes down, just*
>   *missing her. They struggle. She grabs it.*

Cecil Don't touch my chocolate! I knew you'd do that! And no one pulls a fucking knife on me –

Jane Why not?

Cecil You fucking little spoiled cunt – The cheek of it!

Jane No, no, old man – (*She takes control.*) Oh, this is good, good, good. I didn't get it wrong. This is it, all I want –

Cecil What do you want?

Jane To be unafraid of you and of everyone who reminds me of you. So unafraid that I can walk out of here knowing I never have to think of you again. That is the freedom I've come for.

Cecil How will you achieve it?

Jane Get down!

Cecil Leave me! Let me do my eyes. At least let me see to go home. I need water. There's no alcohol in it.

Jane Get your wretched water. But behave. I'm going to see this through.

He fetches water.

Jane I could have drowned myself this morning. Every hour I was being sick. But I bought the knife and found a position at the bus stop across the street, where I made my boyfriend wait years ago, in case I needed him. At last the door opened and it was really you with your plastic bag, coming out to buy your paper and beer. I followed you to the café and waited and then I went in and sat down. I knew you didn't recognise me. Later, in the afternoon, it was the betting shop and café again, where I watched you in the mirror. My best friend from school passed by the window but I couldn't speak, let alone run outside and call to her. To even see your face again had me hallucinating . . . The past is my sickness. I wept for my husband and wished I'd had more time with him. And I wanted to go home.

Cecil What kept you pursuing me like this?

Jane His memory. His voice inside me.

Cecil Could you please pass me the cotton wool? There.

Jane Bernard was politically romantic. He taught me resistance begins in the mind, with speaking to oneself, and then at home, in the kitchen, and it reaches out into the wider world, the dream is reality, man –

Cecil Excuse me.

Jane When he was old he grew his hair again.

Cecil How big was his kitchen?

Jane Sorry? What?

Cecil Who cleaned his kitchens? How many people worked for him? He had people looking at him like Labradors. Bernard was a big man, what was he, fifteen stone, with breasts, massive in every way, you were still a child at twenty-two, suspect he was all over you – it turned my stomach – a vile, monstrous self-indulgent man could –

Jane Don't hold yourself back out of politeness.

Cecil Did he want you to do unusual things? You were always a flirt. To make Esther mad you'd sit on my knee, arms around me, face against mine. Just here.

Jane I think I wanted to find the love in you.

Cecil You were trying out your beauty as the beautiful have to – to see what can be done with it. What it might bring them. Didn't it work well? Esther and I had our own celebration, we cracked open the pale ale and hopped across the room when he asked you to live with him. Like all good parents we knew that while your hair shone and your skin was fresh you had to sell it at the highest price –

Jane Sell it –

Cecil As young women still do, your flesh and mouth his every night. You think you would have walked with him on that red carpet, or shopped on Fifth Avenue, or exchanged talk of the latest films with movie stars and artists in the world's best cafés, if you'd been a fourteen-stone gargoyle with boils? Gargoyles stay home. Why else, but because of Bernard, d'you think, they're giving you an exhibition? Every rich man's wife is an artist in oils. The thing is, I've studied you, Jane, at close quarters and you've always been slightly lazy – You've flitted, never persisted, never seen anything through, you don't know who you are – I always had to push you. Esther and I would talk it over, as we did everything. What it would be like, with Bernard's friends, so full of purpose, ambition, artistic energy . . . And her, not stupid one bit, but lacking that spine of expectation – Did you feel left out?

Jane I'm a keen listener. It compensates for a lot of other social inadequacies, particularly with artists. It was good enough for me to be safe. To live without unnecessary crisis or suffering . . . The peace, the sheer content in the garden I made, trees planted, walks opened up, ponds laid, and in the conservatory where I read, and in the house . . . I'd walk around the rooms singing, loving them and what I intended to do with them –

Cecil Oh Jane, I'm glad you're here: we're going for it all tonight.

Jane Despite your hopes, Bernard and I were always curious about one another. Of course, I looked at younger men, more straightforward guys, less moody, less paranoid. Like everyone I thought of the other lives I could have led, and they always seemed better than the one I had. But I never wanted to be with anyone else. (*Pause.*) I liked to sit with him in his study for days at a time, listening to music, drawing, talking. He was always taking pictures, talking, writing poetry, doing something that made me want to do something. Or he was working on what he called a filthy little thriller . . . about 'the usual', a girl, a man and a gun . . . I guess it was based on some of the things I'd told him.

Cecil It was? He was using you?

Jane We were useful to one another.

Cecil He had the gift, the imagination. Who wouldn't want to be close to that heat? Now it's turned off. What is there for you now? We don't want you to be a professional widow, going round the world saying he worked with the windows open and liked Laurel and Hardy –

Jane No –

Cecil There's no future in the past. You still cause us fret and worry –

Jane I've been cutting myself.

Cecil You have?

Jane You start landslides and explosions in my head, as you always did. Why should I listen to you? I didn't come to discuss Bernard or my father – I mean my future.

Cecil You don't have to, Jane. Let's forget it. Have a drink of water. You're dehydrated.

Jane Yes. I am. I will do that.

Cecil You really are exhausted and unwell in the mental area. You wouldn't rate the guys in the police station, I can tell you, I know them. You could rest here and gather some strength. Killing is hard work. Before you get on with it, lie down. Take off your shoes. I'll help you. I'm ill too, and getting tired. I'm going to lie down myself, nearby.

Pause.

34

I told Esther to be honest about me to you. I didn't want
to be hidden, with her ashamed of me, except she thought
it was the only way she could see us both. Like you,
Esther's always scared. I'd have let her in this evening.
I said you could be made to understand . . . And you can,
can't you?

Pause.

Do you still go to the races? I'd lift you onto my shoulders
so you could see. (Pause.) Have you still got your bicycle?
(Pause.) Remember when we spent all day making that
damn pond in the garden, and the water ran away? What
were the names the old astronomers gave places on the
moon? The Sea of Darkness . . . the Sea of Tranquillity . . .

Jane We'd make them up.

Cecil Lying together on the sofa –

Jane Moon the Obscure . . .

Cecil The Sea of Tea.

Jane Krapp's Last Moon – Moon's Last – (Pause.) 'Ding-
ding, any more fares please!'

Cecil Yeah. You'd sit at the front on the top deck and
go to the end of the route. I'd hear your feet above my
head – That's them, I'd think, the children, enjoying the
ride and the view –

Jane Who am I made of? The dead are never dead and
the walls ooze ghosts . . . our bodies are houses of the
dead . . . we walk about with them inside us, they speak
through our mouths, moving us in directions we don't
want to go . . . Oh Cecil – Stop, please . . .

Cecil I am stopped. But while you're still awake, before
I forget, I wanted to ask you, won't you pay for us to go
somewhere –

Jane What are you saying, Cecil? Who wants to go somewhere?

Cecil Not you this time, girl. You're the lucky one who's been everywhere and back. Mum and I, you know, we want to go to Texas.

Jane You want to go to Texas?

Cecil Near Arizona. They say Esther's in remission, which always means death. They removed the lump and then the breast.

Jane Yes –

Cecil Now the other one has to come off.

Jane It does? Oh.

Cecil So, a last trip out with Esther would be welcome, just the two of us and the sky. Motels, rented Chevvy, roof down, a bit of a smoke, swinging and singing through the canyons and valleys. She'd love that so much, Jane, we both would –

Jane I came to kill you, you cunt, not send you on holiday.

Cecil You're opposed to it, yeah, at the moment. Emily's going to have every chance there is, but no one gave Esther the imagination to see the possibilities out there –

Jane Emily. My daughter. Earlier you said something . . . I almost missed it. You said Emily was bright.

Cecil That was you, the passionate mother, making up for your own mother's mistakes, never leaving the kid alone, pushing education into her, that's why she's anorexic.

Jane What?

Cecil But Esther always says it over and over, Emily's dazzling, she'll make films, run businesses, play professional poker, or was it tennis –

36

Jane Cecil, if you live, I will send you to Texas near Arizona, swinging and singing through the canyons –

Cecil You will? Right. Good. You're Jesus in a dress. Wow!

Jane I'd send you anywhere they have the death penalty. But answer this. Okay? (*Pause.*) Has she been here? My daughter. Did Mother bring her to you? Has she been in this room? Yes?

Cecil All right. Yes.

Jane What . . . what did you say?

Cecil Talkative girl, had her violin, played something, sang, danced, was into everything and told me that something I did was 'so last century'. Puberty comes early these days, or is it just me?

Jane What did you do with her?

Cecil Oh, I think I gave her pizza and Coke. She's family, part of me, too.

Jane No –

Cecil I won't be forced out, forgotten. I was there –

Jane Did you touch her?

Cecil I went through it with this family – I helped out –

Jane Did you?

Cecil Why should I?

Jane Why didn't she tell me? Did you order her not to? Did you coerce my daughter? Or was it Mum?

Cecil I don't want to just touch just anyone! What do you think I am, a pervert? With her I only looked into your eyes again, and was reminded of the love we had. Esther was frantic. She knew it would start me off on the regret and despair and drinking. She had to pull me back to earth before I tore everything apart, before I took myself off to hell! But I told myself, I will not let all this family feeling go to waste! I will hold it together!

Pause.

Jane, look at you, you're worrying now, you get upset at the slightest thing, and you say you've left Emily with your new man friend. They're under the same roof now, tonight, curled up, her sweet face on the pillow, her hair everywhere. And where is he? You say you know him, you trust him, not with your life, but with your daughter, is that right?

Jane I don't know. Nothing stays still. What are you saying?

Cecil I'm saying, d'you understand, you've got to be careful, people don't know themselves what they want. How d'you know it wasn't her he wanted, not you?

Jane What? Did you want us then, or me, not Esther? Is that it?

Cecil I was blind, Jane, knowing nothing, but moving forward. No one over twenty-five is really beautiful – not like that. The young are irresistible, spoiled, oblivious. And the world is saturated with the appreciation of younger and younger physical beauty, with people wanting people for who knows what, to kiss, to explore, to lose themselves in, their eyes and hands over one another, even against their own will, it's all there is and there must be a lot of it about, for people to get so upset about it. It's you who make it odd, strange, unusual, trying to straighten everything out –

Jane You say I can't kill but you might just have got me wrong there –

Cecil You're exactly the damn same as your mother –

Jane That is going to make any daughter kill –

Cecil You know what I want to do? Let's heal, Jane, together, let's pray and heal and forgive and go back to the love, the real love that's really there – On our knees, you and me, asking the only person who can give it, for forgiveness –

He throws the bowl of water in her face, grabs her, snatches the knife and holds it in front of her.

Cecil Let me look at you.

Jane Help –

Cecil Put your face . . . there.

Jane If you hit me –

Cecil Open your eyes.

Jane Don't hit me!

Cecil Open! See me in your eyeballs! There – there I am! Hello! Good! Do what I say now and no one will get accidentally cut up. This is how you hold a knife. Where was I?

He finishes drinking from the first can, opens another and drinks; prepares a third.

Drinking's never been my problem, sobriety is. (*Pause.*) Now we're on. I'm ready. Wallop. (*Pause.*) You're right about something, girl. I'm not Daddy. I'll never be Daddy. Father would be better. Then you apologise for this. (*Pause.*) What would your therapist say if you came home with a scar across there? Think about it. (*Pause.*) Father. I'll explain why. Then you say it nice and loud. Yeah. Father.

Pause.

It is you I notice – you're the one who stands out – the first time I run into the three of you, on the beach. I've been doing up this chalet at Camber. I go there whenever I have spare time and money. But why are you lot there? One of those mad runnings of Esther's, on acid. She's coming down, I find out, not that you know the details. She's always coming down, or going up, never actually hitting the target.

Pause.

It's cold, she's made a fire, you and that boy Jimmy are chucking stupid wet things on. It's all no good, and I fetch you all to my chalet and put you in bed. I look at her, it's a glance, but I can see the light in Esther, running low, but it's on. That night she takes me out into the wind, wants me to see the point of it, what she's been looking at. She's so wild, always zagging when everyone else just zigs! We make love like demons and she says mister, man, couldn't I just do something with you! Something!

She likes a good time, says she's free and careless, except she's got two kids, no job or money, a house full of doped-up bums lying on dirty cushions and her suddenly deciding to hitch-hike to the sea and not even capable of getting the kids to school.

A few weeks in I think I've got to get away from this lot, they'll drag me to the bottom. I was a communist but never a communalist. I've got a friend in the bus garage to talk to. Except he has young children he's always putting to bed. I leave his house and walk away, and I feel lonely, you know, I can even cry. I don't know . . . I don't know what to do.

Pause.

I take you on. An instant family. And I stick with it for a long while. That makes me Father. Father. The one to be hated, but not only that.

Jane You think I don't want to walk in here and put my arms out and say, 'Hello, Daddy, where are you taking me for dinner?'

Cecil Dinner! I come home one night-time, I've sunk a few, right, a working man is entitled, all day I've been driving that 94, and I been paid. I want to see my kids, my family. I've never had it. I'm starting to believe in it. Esther isn't there, of course. Must have been out on one of her attempts to cure herself, once and for all, funny really, but not for me. She's almost impossible to look after, but I can't let her fall back. The boy's there with the neighbours, my Buddy Holly records are all over the place and broken, and he's always going, 'Ding, ding, any more fares please,' though he knows I'm not the conductor. I'm the driver, you have to look where you're going. And you standing there, in boots and green hair, doing stuff to make your eyelashes stick out, ready to go to some boy, and I say, isn't there anything to eat, Jane?

Jane An incitement to murder if ever I heard one –

Cecil We're not your servants, you say –

Jane You're not even our father, you're nothing to us, you're just here all the time, telling us what to do –

Cecil That's why Father has to take off his belt now and again.

Jane I'm bruised . . . I can't go out like this. It hurts when I walk – Look what you've done –

Cecil Sit down and stay in with me tonight – Stay, stay where I can hear your voice . . .

Jane I can't –

Cecil Why not?

Jane No – I have to go forward, there have to be other people –

Cecil Why? (*Pause.*) It's true, you're not mine, you're always in the way, wanting and whining, no one really wants other people's kids. The only people who really like other people's children are paedophiles.

Pause.

And me, Jesus, I've had no training for it, I been in the army, families are worse than wars, the chaos of you wild children and her wanting me to drink and trip out with her, what am I doing . . . there has to be control and discipline – I'm trying to dig out sense and order with my bare hands –

Jane Is that what you were doing?

Cecil (*pause*) Is that a question? It's something I've thought about. Two of you – you an' Mum – have come through singing. That's a decent result.

Jane Sorry, but my therapist says, a cactus in the desert . . . it grows straight and strong for ever if it doesn't get wounded; the branches grow from the place it's been traumatised, it organises around that point . . .

Cecil There are no unwounded. It's terror after terror. But you suffer in particular; your complaints are awful. Who's going to listen to them if they're not paid by the hour? It's very unattractive –

Jane You are so cruel. Have you not noticed that other people are not like this?

Cecil I look up and there you are, stalking me in my local café. Outside, I realise you're following me in the street. I come out of this building later and think, what's the little princess's game, sizing me up through her silly sunglasses minute after minute, hour after hour, waiting. Why can't she come over? Why won't she speak if that's what she's come for? She's making me worried but I wait to find out. At last she gets up; there's a tap on my shoulder. (*Pause.*) You are the ghost, Jane. You say to me, what are you doing here?

Jane I am afraid of you.

Cecil Even now?

Jane Afraid of what you make me feel.

Cecil You say you have some questions so you scare the living shit out of me. But something settles. I begin to ruminate on it, what you really want.

Jane You do? You know that – what I really want?

Cecil You have no husband, no guidance, no meaning, you're all over the place. You got too much money, and the ambition you had to get out and make your own life has run down. It was desperate and powerful but it hasn't been renewed. You've come to me tonight, to ask me, to be told how to get by, how to live more. You know I'm the one to tell you, daughter, because I know you can be better than you have been . . .

Jane Really?

Cecil You have quality of life, daughter, but not quality of love for yourself or anything else. Esther and I have that, we sit here of an evening like jewels in velvet –

Jane Crying with laughter –

Cecil A strange love, an everyday love, doesn't make any sense to the outsider, why should it, and you still want my help –

Jane I do want that. Please give it to me, Father.

Cecil Good.

Jane I will ask you this, Father.

43

Cecil That's the way.

Jane I seem confident, I seem able to walk and talk. But the level of violence that has been in my mind, the shaking, terror and humiliation that I have felt for years, which at times has disabled and ruined me. What could I do with it . . . but put it back into you where it belongs?

Cecil Kill me, then. You could kill me a hundred times. I'm dying anyway –

Jane That's good news, but you won't be saying goodbye with your bollocks stuffed in your mouth as you will tonight –

Cecil One night, I'm dead – say –

Jane Right –

Cecil Let's imagine it –

Jane Yes –

Cecil A game, okay? You're lying in bed, and this anger, it comes back . . . and you still want me out of your mind. You want some peace, some contentment, because you want a perfect father, but it never goes. Aggression just keeps rolling in. Why would it stop? What then?

Jane What would you say, Father, if I were one of the poor exploited and maltreated who still come to you for advice and courage?

Cecil (*he drinks*) You can't think it out of yourself, no. That won't work. You'll go round and round yourself until you go mad. No, you sing of it, like Billie and Bessie and the others. So you take action, using all you know, your art, your experience. You work with children, the damaged like you. You get close to them. The past is your capital. Nothing is wasted then. It all adds up. (*Pause.*) You've **got** the time for several lives.

44

Pause. He gives her the knife.

Take it. I worked with let-down, put-down men. Hearing of my misfortunes gave them hope. They went into action, they did things. Put it away.

He gives her the knife. Then he gives her a pencil.

Draw me instead. You're an artist, here's a pencil, some paper. Before you go, you should do my impression. It'll relieve you. Capture the beast.

Jane Take your shirt off.

Cecil Now that's an invitation! Which is my best side d'you think? The working-class, brutal, violent, ugly . . .

Jane I want to draw the muscle, see if it's as I remember it. The head.

Cecil The old-man stink. They'll love it at the exhibition. Your friends will wonder where you found me.

Jane Your hands.

Cecil Esther and I will come to the opening. She'll be proud of us both. You sure you got enough light?

[He fiddles with the venetian blinds]

Come on! More light you bastard!

He rips the whole thing down. We see the sky and moon.

Hey. Show me someone who understands venetian blinds and I'll show you a human giant, sea of tranquility.

Cecil Halfway down the bus route there was a music shop. I saw a guitar and I parked the bus up, full of passengers. They could wait. I went in, it was a good price, with a book. When I got home you took it upstairs, as Esther and I disputed and had a few cans. We could hear you playing upstairs, just the one chord on and on, and then your voice, singing . . .

Crossfade. Pause.

Jane, please. I ache with cramp. I can't do it any more. I want to see what you've done.

He gets down.

Let me have a look. This is good. Can I have one of these? Can I choose one? In this one you've captured my pain. That's the look of me I want, the wounded bastard in his glory. You've learned a lot from me, but you won't tell them that, I know. I must put this one up here. I've got some drawing pins somewhere. I think they're on that calendar I got from the Chinese restaurant. (*He looks for it.*) Give my regards to Venice. When the pictures are done, please let us come, your family, to peruse the artefacts.

She puts her shoes and coat on.

I will find those cuttings, too. They're in an envelope somewhere. Here. Take them to one of your homes.

She looks through them.

Cecil They're already fading – What would he say if he'd seen you prancing about with that knife, eh? His voice inside you?

Jane Bernard?

Cecil Yeah? What's the old man saying?

Jane He's saying . . . stick it right in the pig with a flag on the end. Hey, maybe I still should, cheer myself up. What d'you think? (*Pause.*) Didn't you say I never persisted –

Cecil I don't know you now, Jane –

46

Jane That I never see anything through but flitted – was that the word you used – flit –

Cecil And you like to play the only injured party, the innocent good girl –

Jane – from thing to thing? It's true my mind has never fixed –

Cecil But you weren't invited here, you barged in and smashed my head. You sent Esther away. Now you can get out of it and leave me, I'm starting to feel not so good –

Jane At school they said, she doesn't concentrate, she's always somewhere else. But it was fear and anxiety –

Cecil I can feel myself turning dark and dirty inside now –

Jane – that kept me from sticking at anything. And behind it all, the Marsh of Corruption . . . The Sea of Fear . . .

Cecil I could take exception to things that before seemed normal – It's in the picture . . . I can see it . . .

She slashes him on the back.

Cecil I was going to say . . . the Texas trip I mentioned earlier . . . is it still on?

Jane Put your shirt on.

Pause.

Cecil You know, out there, in the desert, if we go, we talked of getting married at last.

Jane It's done.

Cecil It might surprise you, but I want to do something decent. Is that going to be all right with you?

The front-door buzzer sounds. Pause.

47

Cecil Jane. She won't have slept. She'll be worried out of her mind. And when she sees me – It's going to start us both off. She's going to have to deal with me now. Don't make me turn her away.

The buzzer sounds again.

Cecil Jane –

Jane You'd better speak to my mother, then.

Cecil Right. Yeah. Okay. (*Into intercom.*) Hallo, Esther, is that you? I'm up here and I'm okay. What are you doing? You coming up? Come on then, girl. The lift's still broken. I'll be here, waiting for you. Yeah, there's been . . .

He pushes the button.

Cecil Go down the other stairs and through the car park.

Jane Goodbye, Cecil.

Cecil Jane –

Jane Enjoy Texas.

She goes.
Cecil puts on a record. He starts to clean up the room. There's a knock on the door. He tidies more hurriedly.

Cecil Esther! Esther, is that you? Daddy's just coming. Hold on . . . just wait there a minute. I'm getting decent for you. We're going to go away together, you know, and get married, like we talked about . . . I'm going to make it happen . . . I've had a busy evening, I'm going to tell you all about it right now!

He opens the door.

Blackout.